The Curiosity of Roadside Attractions:

A Collection of Haiku and Senryu

Jennifer Gurney

ISBN: 978-93-6354-559-5

First Edition: 2025
Rs. 200/-

Cyberwit.net
HIG 45 Kaushambi Kunj, Kalindipuram
Allahabad - 211011 (U.P.) India
http://www.cyberwit.net
Tel: +(91) 9415091004
E-mail: info@cyberwit.net

Printed at Repro India Limited.

Dedication

The Curiosity of Roadside Attractions is dedicated to my son, Travis. Growing up, he was my road trip companion, willingly stopping to see a two-headed cow, foot-high pie, Wall Drug Store and even Car Hedge. Love you, Son. You make the journey of life so much more interesting!

the curiosity of
roadside attractions
magnetic pull to stop

on the
other side of dark
comes the dawn

cracks in the path
lead to
memories of you

hinting at falling
like being in a cloud
spring rain

dusk–
sun turning in
night awakening

one by one
each star appears
my wish suspended

cottonwood branches
broken for you
a star is born

in silent awe
I sit at the feet
of your kindness

only direction
my heart sometimes goes
backward

watching Rear Window
alone in the dark
I scare myself

pocketful of heart rocks
you hike this path
with me

when you were gone
I laid on your bed
hungry for your warmth

hanging in the eaves
just a wink out of view
sadness

windy morning
my cat chases
sunlight shadows

quiet morning
coffee percolating
only sound I hear

writing notes
in the margins
pages of life

on the lake's surface
the sun poses
with the clouds

drifting in silently
like the afternoon cloud bank
sadness

clouds float
in reflection
on river's surface

opera's intermission–
the audience rests
its hearts

I ugly cried
at your funeral today–
rivers of love

doughnuts
in the parking lot–
Michigan winter

eyeball to eyeball
with creativity–
I see you tick

made of stone or cars
still a henge
indubitably

garage sale
or large item pick up
hard to tell sometimes

my rhythms
full moon
waves

hearing the siren
I pull over to the side
whispering a prayer

grief's magnitude
in direct proportion to
love's depth

I love rainy days
when my heart needs a good cry
synchronicity

phantom noises
creaking stairs in empty house
door closing on its own

frog chorus
the bass section
of a lake chorale

no pelicans
the lake seems empty
without you

castles in the sand
last only until
tides turn

now that I'm
writing more
I'm cleaning less

in the pruning
comes
the blossom

if my life were
a museum you would be
my favorite collection

I want to swim
in the water of this grace
forever

twenty eight years
the span of graduations–
blended family

the blue
of your eyes
connects us

love
eclipses
indifference

I freeze this day
to remember
forever

I would know
that melody anywhere–
ice cream truck

I know your every
bend and curve, bump and wrinkle
root and branch, my tree

first star twinkles on
and I raise
my glass of Malbec

inside jokes
so much better
from the inside

floating on the surface
sunlight, gentle waves
memories of love

your hairs cling
to all things black
even after you're gone

in every house
where I've ever lived
lives someone else, now

messy handwriting
on the back of an envelope…
red-light poems

my head in your lap
your fingers in my hair
total contentment

every time
I make a fried egg sandwich
I think of you

shucking corn
in a grocery store bin
anticipation

watermelon sliced
laundry hung on the line
summer morning

flip flops by the door
beach towel on the rail
the lake is calling

when I wake
with an empty to-do list
blissful summer day

I miss dial tones
calling time and temperature
and prank phone calls

set off the fire alarm
in junior high home ec class
burned cinnamon rolls

peeling and peeling
and peeling all day–
orange marmalade

mindfully present
I touch
eternity's wings

conch-shell pink
lifting skyward
ideal morning

your love, a pebble
making infinity-ripples
on my heart

dew drops at dawn
cover the fallen leaves with
diamond light

drifting
on a warm, sandy beach
day dream

softly falls the night
blanketing the world
in quiet calm

subtly
the sky silently sings
in color

even in the dark
of early morning rising–
birdsong wakes the day

long, slow kisses
underneath the stars
good for the soul

just to hear his voice
howling in an empty room
my cat diva

walking in the door
I sometimes, still
call your name

softly, slowly
breath by breath
you fill my day

an empty promise
hangs in the balance
waiting to be filled

delphiniums
against periwinkle sky
lost in blue

the river
floods its banks
with all my tears

grief slides in
through the cracks in my heart
that never fully healed

each morning
I remember
anew

the road ahead
is paved solely by
good intentions

I could write
books of love poems
all about you

first mail arrives
and last box is unpacked–
totality

with you
in my back pocket
life is good

www.ingramcontent.com/pod-product-compliance
Ingram Content Group UK Ltd.
Pitfield, Milton Keynes, MK11 3LW, UK
UKHW041315190726
13845UKWH00025B/293